LES
EBENISTES
DU VIN

LES EBENISTES DU VIN

Jean-Marc Soyez

translated by Michael Mills

photographs by
Jacques Guillard and Jean-Daniel Sudres

EDITIONS
DE LA PRESQU'ILE

If ever a story deserved to begin with the words "Once upon a time...", then it is the story of barrel-making. For on that far-off day when, no doubt enlisting the collective energies of the entire clan, some inspired soul laboured to produce the first barrel, the result must surely have been a success.

For if, after such a concentration of labour, of ingenious skill, of intuition, the thing had simply not worked, the idea would have been abandoned. They must surely have got it right first time. So we can truly say the story of barrel-making did indeed begin once upon a time...

It seems likely, indeed certain, that the original idea which spawned the whole process of barrel-making was simply the plugging of leaks in a dugout boat, using pieces of wood smaller than the actual hole.

This forerunner of the barrel stave would probably have been a sliver peeled from the branch of a softwood tree — like the hollowed-out tree trunk boat and indeed, much later, like the

Acorns and leaves of the oak tree, since remotest prehistory the shining symbol of strength. Chieftains would claim kinship with these immortal giants of the virgin forest

9

barrel itself, all of them natural shapes that compelled the hardworking boatman to put together something that was rudimentarily watertight.

The distant ancestors of the barrel were designed to prevent liquid from coming *in*. It took, no doubt, many generations of skilled and inventive men to turn the equation around and produce objects, or rather receptacles, designed to stop liquid from coming *out*.

Later on they would be called *vaisseaux*, "vessels", which comes from the Latin word *vascellum* meaning receptacle or even, in Roman legion slang, mess-tin.

Modern French still uses the expression *vaisselle vinaire* in connection with the grape harvest. George Sand, who knew how to turn a fine phrase or two, distinguished between the *vaissel de mer* (ship) and the *vaissel de terre* (barrel).

So we have now established that the precursors of the barrel-maker, or cooper, plied dugout boats. These were skilled people and reasonably well equipped. Moreover, their collective memory meant that they could hand down any technical advances. They were contemporary with the first mixed economy (hunting and fishing, gathering, farming), and the domestic economy of their community was a solid one. Unlike more primitive societies, they tended to repair things rather than throw them away.

We know a good deal about these people at the end of prehistory — or, if you prefer, at the dawn of our own era.

We are talking about the Bronze Age, and Celtic tools. The tools would remain essentially unchanged until the invention of the first electric drill. By the beginning of the Iron Age, some three thousand years ago, at the start of what is called the Hallstatt Period, the barrel was in such common use that it already had its place in the popular imagination. This was the age of Silenus,

whom the Romans called Bacchus. Tutor to Dionysus, god of the vine, Silenus was pictured sitting astride either his donkey or his barrel.

In the ancient Argos of Homer, as punishment for murdering their Egyptian husbands, Zeus (Jupiter) condemned the forty-nine daughters of the hapless Danaos to fill a bottomless barrel with water from the Tartarus — a symbol still widely familiar today. And then there was Diogenes, sickened at being unable to find a real man by the criteria of the philosophy of the Cynics: he withdrew from the world to live in a barrel, that most humble of all shelters.

The Romans knew all about barrel-making, but had fewer echoes in their mythology. Julius Caesar is the first to mention the barrel,

Cousin to the stave-maker, his contemporary the hoop-maker leads a solitary life not from choice, but because transporting the chestnut branches to town would eat into his profits

11

and rather indignantly at that, in his commentaries on the wars in Gaul. He recounts that, during the siege of Uxellodunum (the present-day Vayrac, in the Lot) in 51BC, the Gauls rolled a whole lot of old barrels down onto the Roman assailants, filled with "consuming fire" — no doubt burning pitch and tow. This military invention seems to have caused him some inconvenience.

We know that the wine of Aquitaine which was sent to quench the thirst of Claudius's troops during the conquest of Britain in the late 40s BC was transported in barrels — revolutionary in an age when the transport and questionable storage of wine were linked to the amphora.

14

Nero may have been mad, but he certainly had a nose for a juicy tax opportunity. In the Rome of his day they used human urine (the best there is) for bleaching linen. The emperor commissioned the barrel-makers of Rome, and in particular the newly arrived Gaulish coopers, to make special tubs fitted with handles for carrying. These were installed all over the city and carefully guarded, with instructions to Rome to relieve itself in them and nowhere else. Nero, the great urine collector, then either taxed each user or sold the result in bulk to the laundries of Rome — at this point history is a little unclear. It was a thriving industry, if a disgustingly smelly one. As Pliny the Elder so pithily observed, it

To the sound of the birds and the whispering breeze, he patiently constructs his crowns, known, when ready to go to the barrel-maker, as clamps

15

was this that inspired Nero to say, "Money has no odour".

From this time on village barrel-making, here in France a Gallo-Celtic affair, was in a state of continual development, becoming something of an industry. But it never lost its essential artisan quality, which has typified it over the centuries.

From the fourth century AD, barrel-making became a thoroughly Christian affair: coopers turned out vast baptismal vats in which priests could baptise catechumens by total immersion.

You may be amused to learn, if you did not already know, that Charlemagne was as fussy about the upkeep of his *vaisselle de vendange* as he was about his cellar; to the extent that for his entire life he had three German master-coopers attached to his person, with the rank of officer.

Since when, apart from a few naturally or locally inspired innovations, nothing has really changed in the vast domain of barrel-making.

By the end of the nineteenth century, no less than seventy different crafts were carried out using tools developed by master-coopers and their workmen. In Bordeaux a cooper was a *carpentey de barrico*, or barrel-carpenter. In Paris he was a *maître fustier*. And in Burgundy, where they like a good laugh, people descended from barrel-makers often have names like Boivin, Bovin, or Botvin, without any idea of the meaning. They all come, of course, from *boite à vin* or "wine-box", a twelfth-century nickname for the cooper.

To get a rough idea of the everyday significance of barrel-making in the days before white metal or galvanised iron were readily available, let alone today's plastics, we must appreciate that any kind of receptacle not made of terra-cotta or porcelain was in effect a "barrel". Daily use was made of troughs, of tubs and vats, of bowls and basins, of containers for sulphating vines, milk and

Just as in any fairy story, it all begins in the depths of the forest: mysterious signs left by an elf, just glimpsed on bark that has hardly changed for a hundred and fifty years

16

butter churns, wine-jugs, kegs of all kinds, floating buoys for shipping, bidets, pans and scalding-tubs, drainers, funnels, washbowls, gourds and cups, pails and buckets, pitchers, dyer's vats, vases and vinegar pots, primitive washing machines, incubators, and so on.

Messmer's celebrated tubs were born of the skill of a Parisian master-cooper named Tauzin who could interpret the great German therapist's wishes by making him straight cylindrical containers more than two metres tall.

The military master-coopers were not lacking in inventiveness, either. First, there was the *baril d'artifice*, in use for four hundred years, a reminder perhaps of the Gauls of Vayrac. This was a truly infernal machine consisting of four or five small, very thick barrels lashed together and linked by an axle that turned two larger-diameter wheels for rolling the apparatus at the enemy. The barrels were all packed with powder and shot, and a wick passed along the axle.

Then there was the *baril foudroyant*, also very thick and packed with powder, with a wick. It weighed anything from ten to twenty-five kilos, and was thrown at the enemy. Sometimes it was buried under stones, when it was known as a *fougasse*, the forerunner of the anti-personnel mine.

Nor should we forget the eminently peaceful canteen-barrel which, in 1800, Napoleon's troops tied round the necks of the large dogs at the Saint Bernard monastery.

The troublesome powder-keg was used for transporting gunpowder to the battlefield, and in particular to warships. A royal decree of Louis XIV, dated 18 September 1686, laid down the dimensions of the powder-keg. This piece of essential legislation was of course simply the confirmation of what was already in effect as a result of experience and accidents.

Not tree-felling, but tree-harvesting . And not of oak, but of oaks, each different from the next - just like people: a new, unspoken truth

19

Louis XIV's powder-keg was to contain 100 pounds of gunpowder and to be two foot two inches high. The bottom was to be eleven inches and nine lines across, and the diameter at the "bulge" was to be one foot two inches. Carefully hooped in wood, bound with osier, the keg was placed inside a second barrel a few centimetres larger, itself encased in wood as proof against sparks — although this did not prevent often dreadful accidents. The standard powder-keg was still in service under Napolon III.

Nor should we forget the gigantic vats used in cannon (and bell) foundries, and in the newly-emerging heavy industry, for making the first railway lines and the first locomotives. Many of them were still in use at the start of World War Two.

Need we examine further this impressive list, to claim that our civilisation is very largely built on barrel-making?

But just exactly what is a barrel?

In the ancient crafts practised down the ages by craftsmen whose languages were developing, paradox and confusion can themselves become tradition. Thus, our coopers make mostly casks. True, we also require barrels and vats; but we shall see later just what the not inconsiderable differences are. For now, the cask.

According to the best authority, a cask is a wooden receptacle of cylindrical, double-truncated shape with two identical round ends, and is made of braced strips or sections bound by wooden or metal hoops. This unexceptionable description is rather like the one the schoolboy provided of the cat: an animal with a tail, two hind feet, two front feet, two left feet and two right.

Not to keep you in the dark any longer on such a warmly described matter, know that a good three thousand years later the mathematicians of the last century finally discovered the barrel for themselves and rushed to set down a formula for its capacity

And no two staves will ever be exactly the same, either. The great skill is to make them into a perfect whole

that everyone could grasp easily. For example, the capacity of a barrel is identical to that of a cylinder whose height is equal to the interior length of a barrel, AD, and whose diameter, BF, is that of the widest point, EC, reduced by one-third of the difference between the bilge diameter and the diameter of each end, BF.

Of course none of this staggering logic has ever been heard around a cask-maker's workshop. In the face of such blatant lack of faith in their ponderous computations, the mathematicians renewed their attack. They now proposed to multiply the diameter at the widest point by four, or perhaps by the diameter of the end multiplied by eight times the length — how about that? Such wise men are always with us, indefatigable, accustomed to ministry research or, better, ministry panaceas concocted in stuffy offices, to be prudently ignored until the next handout of received wisdom.

In fact the formulas are accurate, at least to within two or three percent. A miserable five to seven litres per cask which, one need hardly be told, would warm the heart of the producer of a *grand cru* or a priceless *eau-de-vie*. Could the wine trade be synonymous with meanness?

Be that as it may, cask-making, a living art if ever there was one, holds itself on principle apart from the threats of the exact sciences. The finished cask has always simply been weighed, empty, and then weighed again when it is full. This of course gives its exact capacity, which is then branded onto the wood. The procedure is sometimes different today, but we are not there yet. As long as cask-making was a strictly manual business, in other words with a healthy dose of empiricism, no two casks ever had exactly the same capacity.

And so, we finally come to the cask.

Laid out flat, a cask looks a bit like a sad handful of planks and

The universe of the staves, these long, tightly packed walls. Or perhaps a sort of hive where, for a thousand days and nights, the wood changes in all kinds of ways (following pages)

23

After being such a safe haven for young fish in calm waters, could this river reed guess why it too has been summoned?

chestnut withies — and makes you realise just how frantically hard a cooper has to work. But this is only a superficial first glance, that of the tourist, as it were. A closer look at these thick pieces of wood reveals that each stave has been meticulously shaped, sanded and finished, and swells slightly towards the middle. Broadly, the finished stave is shaped like a long spindle, but with both ends chopped off. The swelling gives the celebrated mid-cask "bilge" that we hear so much of in barrel-making. The bilge represents an enormously long line of architects and geometricians that by no means began with Euclid and Pythagoras. Any anthropologist will agree that the Achaeans, the Celts and the Galatians share the same origin, although they may not always agree on either its name or its geographical location. It is not up to us to decide here. But one historical fact remains: these post-Neolithic invaders were extremely well-versed in geometry and architecture, which of course means in mathematics as well. Of the many examples, a particularly poetic one serves to illustrate these skills. The architects of the Parthenon knew that if the columns were exactly parallel then, when looked at from below at the level of the faithful masses, the temple of Athene would look a bit like a gingerbread cottage. So they put their heads together and corrected the sight lines, allowing the building to swell out a little up to cornice level, so that it would look perfectly square-set against the heavens of the gods.

The less sophisticated but equally astute Gauls knew the secret of building a bridge on moving piles, to enable them to cross a river no matter how high or low the water level.

The cask's "bilge" uses exactly the same idea. It took astonishing skill to realise that, multiplied by the number of staves required (30-odd for the average cask), a gentle linear swelling would give that most resistant of all shapes, the dome. In this case, an endless dome-shape — an amazing concept. For it is when it is lying down, in its true position, that the cask demonstrates its remarkable qualities: the entire mass rests on a few square millimetres. We do not know what word the Gauls gave to this stroke of genius. But our more recent forebears called it, quite simply, the *bouge* (or "bilge" in English) because it meant that even a child could manoeuvre a full 350-litre cask with one hand.

The next time you see a cask think of the *bouge*, that extraordinary piece of pre-Hellenic mystery. It will not prevent you from sampling, in advance, the boons of the contents; and you will be in a better position to drink deep from this work of art, complex and venerable as it is.

It all began in the forest

As we dig deeper into this profound subject, it is worth going back to the lowest common denominator, as it were: the vast Neolithic forest. And, while we are at it, let us take the opportunity to have a quick look at the story of our, your, forest.

Trees: a brief history

At some point in the high, far-off past, certain little algae that looked more like slime than moss attached themselves to rocks on the seashore and managed not to die when the tide went out.

What extraordinary notion impelled them to desert the life-giving waters of the sea? And instead of drying out, by what mysterious means did they manage to survive and then grow? We do not know.

Without flowers, roots, blood-vessels or skeletons, they must have made up for their extreme fragility by being amazingly fertile. All this apparently took place some six hundred million years ago, in the era which the experts call the Cambrian or, more precisely, the Ordovician or Palaozoic. In any case, fed on sunshine and rainwater our algae proliferated to such a point that their myriad carcasses formed the first humus. On it, they confirmed the first fruits of the desire to evolve that is common to all living species. Accordingly, then, they developed the peristome, the toothed crown which enables the operculum or lid of a moss to detach itself from the ascidium or capsule. And inside the peristome came the first hesitant appearance of tiny fibrous canals — made of wood! These were microscopic passages along which passed a rudimentary lymph fluid, the ancestor of sap. The set-up was complete. It was now only a short step to the dwarf fern, in the shape of the rhynia, a primitive bracken plant 20 to 50 centimetres tall. The rhynia had the beginnings of a fibrous skeleton and double-flow passages for life-giving fluids to irrigate the farther parts. Logical necessity soon required the development of roots — although "soon" is a relative term: this step took some two hundred million years.

All this occurred in the middle of the Primary Era. But we now come to a 58-million-year period known as the Devonian, which saw the birth of the seed - an astonishing device which enabled life to be held in storage.

With amazing promptness, or in other words over several million years, giant horsetails (genuine arborescent ferns as opposed to seed ferns) were reaching out toward the sunlight, that common denominator of all vegetable life. They grew up to fifty metres from the ground where the humus was thickening, the warm half-darkness teeming with primitive insects and the beginnings of reptiles and batrachians, among spongy trunks two metres across. With no very apparent transition the Carboniferous Era started, a

The master cooper's infallible eye calmly shapes edge and bilge, trims staves to just the right length. The barrel is born

journey that was to last sixty-five million years. The ferns were joined by the sigillaria, by thirty-metre high lepondendrons with enormous trunks, by ondonpterides and calamites, the first palm-trees, by walchias, and then by the gingko, ancestor of the conifer and the oldest of the trees we know today. This marked the end of the Primary Era, to the accompaniment of the telluric chaos that engulfed great areas of this ebullient forest that was to become what we know as coal.

The Secondary Era began with a brief, thirty-million-year period during which the palm-tree established itself in a form very similar to what we know today. It was "quickly" followed by the nobility of the Jurassic Period, the heyday of the woltzia, the gingko, the cypress, the araucaria or monkey-puzzle tree, the sequoia pine (at

120 metres the tallest tree ever known), the spruce and so on — altogether some twenty thousand species, of which only about six hundred survive. The Jurassic Period ended around 140 million years ago. Almost all the plant forms were still extant, although in varying degrees of density. A radical change was marked with the arrival of the flower. The first flowering tree was the magnolia. We may reasonably suppose that this "invention" coincided with the first bees. It was followed by the explosion of leafed trees which covered the end of the Secondary Era.

There thus appeared, over only a few dozen thousand years and in forms identical to those we know them by, the poplar, the willow, the oak, the elm, the eucalyptus (a hundred metres tall), the beech, the ash, the birch. The plane tree marked the start of

The staves must not only be properly "married" to make an efficient, long-lasting barrel: today, with wineries open to public inspection, they must also be carefully graded

required for soils to stabilise and for trees to take root once more, we must accept that the natural forests of Europe are very recent. The spruce stands are a bare 3,000 years old, the fir forests 5,000, and the vast oak forests that covered ancient Gaul are hardly more than 6,000 years old.

In terms of the history of tree genetics, we are at the beginning of the natural expansion of the forest. Without man's sometimes disastrous interference, the forest would cover all of earth's land surfaces in less than two centuries. Two centuries: hardly the blink of an eye in the long course of the history of the tree (see *Histoire de la Forêt Française* by the same author, published by Editions Denoël).

TIME-HONOURED CRAFTSMANSHIP

Like his alter ego the master carpenter, the master barrel-maker or cooper allowed his wood to be selected by no one but himself.

The adventure of the cask thus began with a trip into the forest, a long one or a short one depending on how far away the workshop was — but always a painstaking one. The cooper's reputation depended on his choice of "barrel tree", as did those of all the craftsmen in turn dependent on him.

Different end-uses often required different woods. Oak and chestnut, with their high tannin content, were suitable only for wines, liquors and vinegars. But they would have ruined butter or meat, casks for which were made of rot-proof, odourless acacia. Kegs for fish were made of poplar, not only odourless but also highly salt-resistant. White birch was used to store paper, cloth and valuable material. For miscellaneous purposes ash would do, or willow, or alder, "which costeth naught". For certain "medicinal" baths, eucalyptus was used. Pine or fir-wood was

A trick of the light, or a clever photographer? The barrels become ghostly, slender, like something in a Cubist painting

36

used for troughs, buckets, hods, and casks for containing tar, pitch, collophane, and so on. Linden-wood was the basis for a highly specialised prosthetics industry that turned out such things as corsets, leg-reinforcers and splints.

The master-cooper marked his trees, indicating the size of the "balks" for each, or where the "billets" should be cut. He then returned to his workshop, and the woodcutter or the stave-maker (in fact often the same trade) took careful note and set to work.

The trees were felled and cut into lengths with a two-man saw (leaving a little extra margin for safety). The woodcutter then changed hats and became the stave-maker. He was a strange beast of the forest, living and working alone with his billets. He would build a little hut in which to live from late autumn until late

spring, by which time he would have filled his orders.

The stave-maker always worked fresh, green wood. He first split his billets star-fashion in quarters, using iron wedges and following the grain of the wood.

Each quarter then became a "doubloon", so-called because it was itself again split in two to give the basis of the barrel stave. The tool used was the cooper's "divider", a sort of blunt chisel knocked in with a hefty mallet blow, again following the grain.

The stave-maker then used a solid, three-legged frame fitted with a clamp (known since the French Revolution as a guillotine). He used a hatchet with a counter-balancing handle to shear off the doubloon's heart and sap-wood. Thus reduced, the doubloon was then planed down with a two-handed flat plane, to give a

The workshop disappears for a moment, to become the stage of a magic theatre. Delicate ballerinas dedicated to fire - it all smacks almost of Berlioz

39

$1^{1}/_{2}$-inch plank — the stave. When sold or being made up, the stave was always and still is counted by the "quart". Thus: three hundred staves plus two hundred bottom pieces (two bottom pieces equalling one stave) to the quart meant four hundred staves, the quantity needed to make up ten barrels, requiring in theory the working of between five and six cubic metres of knotless-wood billets.

His work done, our semi-hermitic stave-maker would go to collect his pay and then head for home. All things considered, he made quite a reasonable living. For once he was home, he was at leisure to ensure his succession and attend to his house. In fact stave-makers were renowned for their fine houses and their numerous children. There were those who whispered that the latter were more due to the long absences, but who are we to take sides? One thing they certainly did was to tell elaborate stories involving wolves and forests and witches, which they had time to dream up in the depths of the woods. These stave-makers' yarns must surely have inspired such people as the Brothers Grimm and Perrault, among others.

When he "took his pension", in other words retired, a stave-maker was the only manual labourer who, if possible, did not end up being supported by his children. He would frequently become a "connoisseur" or herbalist, or else clerk to a pharmacist or doctor who would find invaluable the knowledge of plants that he had acquired.

The staves remained in the forest, to be carried to the cooper's shop by mule (there being of course no roads). There the quarts were set to dry out "in all weathers" for a minimum of three years, to "wash out" all the sap.

For areas where there was much call for barrels but which were far from the forests, such as the Cognac and Bordeaux regions,

Fire, wood, tools: the stage is set, in this theatre where the curtain rises every morning

the staves were made in bulk to standard dimensions in the oak forests of the Limousin. They were then taken by mule to the nearest port on the Charente, often a mere jetty. There were middle-men to take charge of it all. Flat-bottomed boats known as gabarres ferried the staves downstream to workshops located conveniently close to the river. The gabarres were small for Angoulême, Châteauneuf, Jarnac and Cognac, larger for Bordeaux.

This was mere coastal navigation, but a long journey nonetheless, and it unfolded like a sailor's song.

What could be more pleasant, more moving, than to leave the languorous waters of the Charente and enter the Antioch Narrows, so evocative of the Crusades? In bad weather they took

42

the Breton Narrows, no one daring to attempt the short-cut via the Maumusson Strait. The coastal route took them past the islands of Ré and Oléron, skirting La Mauvaise, slipping between the Cordouan sandbanks, to come billowing up the magnificent Gironde. Favourable tides and a following wind meant that within three days they would cast anchor off the Saint Michel district of Bordeaux, where the *carpenteys de barrico* had their work-benches and vices at the ready.

These stave-carrying boatmen had little taste for the open sea. But they were second to none at gliding smoothly between the worst sandbanks. And they would bring back from Bordeaux not only a few choice casks — tax-free of course — to the notables of the Charente, but also barrels of low-quality wine long past

Staves are tough, and bending them is no easy task. The tree is still living and must be tamed - a mystical conflict that confers on the cooper something of the elegance of the matador

43

Once the beast is out of breath, it must be bent and rapidly fastened before it can stretch out again. The steel band is reminiscent of the cowboy's lasso

drinking, which they would sell to the "wine-burners" of Tonnay Charente.

The *carpenteys* set the staves to dry further, in great long lines along the Garonne. And here our solitary, romantic stave-maker is finally lost to sight in this squared-off, geometrically precise image. A man could not be a stave-maker for long without some recourse to poetry. Now it was truly the turn of the barrel-maker.

AND THE STAVE WAS MADE AND IT WAS GOOD

Over three long years of rain, wind and sun, the stave changed. The veins of the wood had tightened, the sap had all been expelled. But in hardening, the fibres retained and distilled the

thousand mysterious savours of the wood — tannin, secret flowers, minute mosses, forgotten but still present.

All that was needed now was the hand of the craftsman, or rather the artist, to crown and glorify all this inexplicable, marvellous alchemy. Once the three or four years were up, the cooper weighed up his sample stave with hand and eye. The language may have varied, but the satisfaction was the same along the Garonne or the Charente, the Rhône or even the Rhine. The stave was pronounced good. Enter, now, another remarkable character, the skiver.

The skiver was nothing like the stave-maker. Indeed, although he was a team member of the same craft, he was just about the opposite.

The inexorable tightening of the second circular mould shackles the staves for ever (following pages). Wagnerian thunder for the barrel-makers' dance, as they hammer on staves four times as old as themselves

Herculean and boisterous, the skiver was as unlettered as his colleagues, a shadowy character if ever there was one, but with an infallible eye. It was his job to use a special cooper's axe or skive to give the stave its final form.

The skive was an axe, but not just any axe. Of extremely antique origin, it was a hefty size: the iron blade alone was over a foot long and would often weigh more than ten kilos.

It was with this redoubtable, highly efficient cutting blade, the wide-ended handle resting on his upper leg, that the skiver strained as he produced results almost worthy of the deft fingers of a lacemaker. His skill lay in shaving the two sides of the wood to give the stave its final form.

His skill also lay — and this was the essential part — in respecting the grain of the wood. Indeed it was from the skiver's work that the grain was known as the *maille* or "bilge". There were large numbers of these skivers, and they would also work for carpenters and cabinet-makers. This explains the slight traces of skiving on the undersides of boards and panels that can still be seen today in very old pieces of furniture.

The emperor Charlemagne was of course as illiterate as any skiver. But he left almost as many documents behind him as the Roman emperors whom he tried so hard to emulate. In particular he drew up one of his famous "capitularies" listing the various tools that were essential for his private barrel-makers. The skive figures prominently, and the details seem to suggest that it was descended from the Salian Frankish battle-axe.

Once they had been properly skived, the staves still required finishing. And this was where the cooper himself took over, trimming them all to uniform length, using plane and "guillotine" to round them slightly. He had a "reverse cutter" for hollowing out the inside face, to make it easier to centre the staves.

Each stave was then "pointed" or tapered at each end, and it was this operation that determined the bilge.

But even now the work was not done. The sides or "profiles" had to be worked, as did the bilge line : only this would give a perfect fit and make the barrel watertight. The cooper used a tool called a *coulombe*, a large plane set on two feet. The staves were ready, but before being assembled they now had to be "fitted", or arranged in pairs, one wide and one narrow, for balance and to make the barrel good and solid. The widest stave of all would become the *douve* or plug-stave, where the bung-hole would eventually be drilled. We do not really know why the French word *douelle*, "stave", turned into *douve* at this point, but it did.

The cooper then collected his staves and set them up vertically in the right order, side by side in a circular form. This was originally made of wood, but from the late fifteenth century was usually metal. As soon as the wooden mallet hammered the last stave into place, the fledgling barrel stood on its end like the petals of some elegant flower. It was then set over a small woodchip-burning brazier, which sprang into life with the arrival of this unexpected chimney.

The staves slowly warmed. An assistant continually swabbed them inside and out with a wringing-wet cloth, at the same time keeping the fire stoked.

Meanwhile the cooper was making the circular form as tight as possible. He then wrapped a special cable around the open "petals", which he tightened with a large-handled screw.

Once the staves had closed up at the bottom, the barrel was taking shape. Before removing the cable, the cooper now hammered home a second circular form.

He then took rapid measurements of the various circumferences of his new barrel, calling them out to the hoop-makers — often a

The circles do as the hammer and punch tell them, literally shaping the new destiny of each stave. Never again will the wind whisper through the branches or even the stave stacks. The shell is now formed, although it is still not a barrel (following pages).

49

band of apprentices under a master, in the adjoining workshop.

Until the eighteenth century, the hoops were usually made of chestnut, trimmed down for about a foot at each end to make a perfect fit before being secured in place with osier. There was no stinting on how many they used; what mattered was effectiveness. In the Cognac area, for instance, they used up to sixteen per cask, eight each side of the bilge — a kind of indestructible corset covering more than half the barrel's surface. Once metal was in common enough use, the hoop-makers would have their own little forge. The hoop would be hammered into shape, and then cut and riveted.

The hooping process, metal or wood and often both, now began. The master-cooper put the first hoop on, using mallet and punch to fit it so tightly that he could then knock free the two circular forms.

After that, the hoops seemed almost to fit themselves. Faster and ever stronger hammer-blows secured them strictly parallel. The punch went round and round, the cooper using his eye, his hammer, his mallet in a harmony of movement and a thunder of noise, as he circled his handiwork. Indeed it was known as the *danse du tonnelier*, the "barrel-maker's dance".

And what a dance it was! After all those years of rustic maturing, lazily following the turning seasons, the barrel was finally born amid an absolute frenzy, in clouds of steam and smoke and flames glinting off skilled hands, muscled arms, tense faces and attentive gazes, all in a clamour of endless thunder. The tranquil forms of the light-coloured wood became, for a time, terrifying wardrums sounded by capering spirits.

Everything finally calmed down again and, in a new-found though relative silence, it was time for the final fitting. This was where the barrel would get its two ends.

52

The magic accomplished,
alchemy takes over. A
shadowy, secretive business
of life-giving fires concealed
in slow burning hearths

First the barrel was placed in a sort of wooden or metal cradle, to hold it at an angle, the open end tipped towards the cooper, who then proceeded to make a bevelled edge or chamfer around the inside edge. To do this he used a special cutting tool called a howel, like a short-handled chisel with a wide, curved blade. Next came the "chime", a kind of groove just below the chamfer, which ran right round the bottom and into which the end would be fitted. To make the chime, the cooper used what was called a "stockholm", a plane of a very special shape which enabled him to work almost without being able to see. The name might lead one to suppose that the tool was invented by Swedish barrel-makers, if such ever existed; but in fact it comes from the origin and quality of the steel blade itself. Before Swedish steel arrived on the scene, the tool was called simply a *jabloir* or chimer.

The barrel was assembled and chimed, and now came the moment for the ends to be mounted. Each end was made of half-staves — always an odd number, seven or nine. The longest ones in the middle were the "mains", and those on each side were the "braces" — *aisseliers* in French, meaning "armpits", a surprising indication of some sort of ancient Celtic symbolic parallel between the circular barrel-end and a magical representation of the human form. The parallel continued intact, and was carried even further by the names of the two arc-shaped pieces that closed the circle: the *chanteaux*, a word of such antique origin that Caesar's legionnaires used it as part of their barrack-room slang (what we know as "low" Latin) as the word *canthum*, meaning corner or edge, and in particular a man's elbow, and thence by extension the part of a shield that protected the elbow.

Latin experts agree that the origin of the word *canthum* is unknown — and who are we to doubt them ?

Anyway, this orphan of a word, the *chantel* of Philip Augustus, is

Witches' cauldrons, or
perhaps veritable athanors
complete with mysterious
recipes. It is not the
philosopher's stone that
they are after, but the
rediscovered savours of
forgotten fragrances
(following pages)

54

bung-boring auger, a large gimlet of a tool. This was extremely sharp, had a large horizontal handle and was turned like any bradawl or drill.

Some barrels and casks were also fitted with extra hoops, close to the bilge, for rolling. Coopers disagreed widely on the helpfulness of this additional precaution.

With or without these rolling hoops, the fresh cask had only one more ordeal to undergo: being filled with two or three buckets of boiling water.

It was turned about in every direction and thoroughly rolled around, to build up enough pressure to reveal any fault. In the process, the inside was also washed clean of the shavings and dust accumulated from the assembly process.

Emptied and stood upright, each barrel now had the cooper's personal mark stamped on its top, above a main stave. There was sometimes a simple attestation added, like this one found on a hogshead in a wine storehouse at Blaye : "Fait par moy, Anselme Graslyer ce vintième de may 1719". The urgency with which barrels were habitually put together apparently had no aesthetic or supernatural cause but was not, as we have already seen, entirely innocent.

The main reason was the desire to get rid (the term is not too strong) of the finished barrel before it dried out too much. All vineyard owners and wine traders of course re-steeped the staves in hot water — or cold, there were two schools of thought. But if a barrel over-dried before it was used, especially in hot weather, then major repair work would have to be undertaken — and preferably at the customer's expense. This meant that barrel-making was never done in advance, but strictly to order and for immediate delivery.

The making of the huge barrel-shaped vat required specialised team-work, closer to that of the carpenter than of the cooper.

It had huge staves, often the size of a medium-sized roof-beam and several metres long, and had no bilge. The ends were slightly tapered instead to give the truncated shape.

It was assembled once in the workshop and then dismantled, to be reassembled again from the bottom up once delivered. Hooping was done on the spot — no mean affair. This giant vat was immovable. Its capacity could vary from ten to a thousand hectolitres or more. The lid could not be removed, and there was a trap for cleaning let in to the top or the side.

Daily life in the simple past

In the manner of other "old time" craftsmen, barrel-makers worked from dawn until the sounding of the Angelus — the unchanging rythm which seemed as natural as drawing breath. In common with most others, they ate where they worked. They did however eat rather better, no doubt because it was easier for them to have a constant fire going and because they earned more than many people.

Like all workers of the day, they complained about the excessive number of non-working holy days, which interrupted their work and interfered with their earnings.

The zealous presence of the barrel-makers at the "anti-holiday" demonstrations, though, was a piece of the purest hypocrisy. For the huge barrel-making *mestié* or fraternity was the only one with more than one patron saint.

It is worth opening a parenthesis here on this word *mestié* or trade-guild. For, unlike other trades, barrel-making was not always controlled by a complex system of corporations, but sometimes by a brotherhood with simple rules which did not insist

Offstage from the ballet, the wings are crowded, shadowy and tense: no flower must be allowed to miss its entrance (following pages)

63

on "masters" and "apprentices" with the limits and frequent nepotism that these involved.

In Bordeaux, for instance, there was never a barrel-makers' corporation, no "master" system, no *jurade* or board of notables, nothing. "Any man who thinks he can work, for his own profit or for another, may set up his workshop without further formality beyond paying the normal taxes". Liberty and common sense were two terms never taken in vain around Bordeaux. It was an attitude that concerned many people. In 1762, there were 317 heads of family who "did practise as *carpenteys de barrico* and did pay tax thereon". If we take into account the families, the assistants and the apprentices, we find nearly as many people in barrel-making as in boat-building.

Free men, then, the *carpenteys* of Bordeaux lived and worked in the Saint Michel district. They honoured the archangel Michael every September 24th, by way of celebrating the imminent grape-harvest. They were also particularly fond of Saint Joseph, whose feast day is on 19th March, but they put it off until the first of May.

In the Cognac region things were more serious. There were corporations with their strings of masters, foremen and companions, and the prestigious Tour de France. The patron saint was John the Baptist, fêted on 24th June, but of course they could hardly ignore either Michael or Joseph — how could they slight Bordeaux so?

In Anjou and Burgundy, in Alsace and around Rheims, the patron saint of the barrel-makers was also John the Baptist. But, like their Cognac colleagues, they also had the courtesy to fête the saint to whom the nearest cathedral was dedicated, as well as those of neighbouring trade corporations.

In Germany and Czechoslovakia, great barrel-making countries

"Rushing", or pulling a river reed, using three fingers to flatten it on a lath. An image as old as history, that deserves a mention in an anthropological treatise

Assembly of the ends looks deceptively simple. The half-staves are prepared before the bilge line

with organised corporations among the oldest in Europe, Saint Nicholas was the preferred patron, without of course forgetting John the Baptist and various others. For these hard-headed, sensible folk saw little sense in wilfully depriving themselves of the benefits of a Saint duly certified elsewhere.

It goes without saying that for a long time, right across Europe, all of these gifted workers, these masters of the cooper's art, took advantage of their naturally close acquaintance with dealers in wine and "other strong liquors" — the term used for *eau-de-vie* — to supply free, with devotion and generosity, the necessary libations for these duty-bound celebrations. Provosts' reports from a number of towns in Europe speak of the "affrays" occasioned by the disturbing piety displayed by *carpenteys*, barrel-

makers and other *Weinküferhandwerker* in the course of their devout observances.

OF TANKARDS AND MUGS, OF VELTES AND ROQUILLES

We sometimes find it a little hard to understand, today, quite what Revolutionary craze for uniformity drove the Thermidoriens, at their great Convention of 3rd April 1795, to impose on France the metric and decimal system. It was to supplant for ever the older method which was at least empirically sound, evolved in the various corners of Europe and no least in France itself.

Despite the turmoils of war and the ravages of the marauding "Compagnon" bands, not to mention pilgrimage — indeed

69

Hardly more decorative than a chicken-house door, the assembled barrel end waits for the cooper's compass to outline its final shape (previous pages)

that. Within a few decades, the last village barrel-makers vanished, their place taken by builders who put up concrete vats everywhere, sometimes ceramic-lined, particularly where quality products were lacking.

As one might expect, the Second War produced no major improvement. Many people were to be more than surprised to find how many little *vins du patron* there were, prettily labelled and appealingly bottled, which had never seen the inside of a barrel or a vat, and perhaps not even a vine either.

The cooper's art had already been stripped of its domestic-appliance aspect, from wooden jugs to bowls. Save in rare privileged areas, it was virtually dead.

The newly liberated chemists now pursued their most evil inclinations. Anyone who did French military service in the 1950s will have an unpleasant memory of the notorious powdered wine that was tested on his tender stomach. There was no more talk of a simple slump: everyone realised that the end was near.

Economic progress, however, helped by generally lazy taste-buds, led to a hesitant, wondering rediscovery of high-quality produce kept in barrels. The decline was reversed, yielding to a renewed and desperate need for barrels — not exactly a test-tube birth, but nearly. And we are currently living through the triumphal wave of this renaissance.

BARREL-MAKING TODAY

But, while all this has been going on, what has happened to the forests, our forests? For if there is no forest there is no wood, which means no barrels.

Our forests are in much better health than they were just over a century ago. One of Charlemagne's famous capitularies tells us

In a chiaroscuro
reminiscent of a Dutch
interior, the cooper selects
the finest stave to drill the
bung-hole

A craft of constant beauty.
Myriad barrel shapes,
light-coloured and round,
each bung bulging out like
a navel in a painting by
Delacroix
(following pages)

79

Skilful planing, the final
act of preparation for the
true birth of the barrel
(previous pages)

final verdict. The dried staves are then taken off to the second shaping shop. The skiver has been replaced by the electric plane. Here again, the difficulty of a major operation has been reduced to almost nothing by the use of a simple machine. And anyway, who would or could accept, today, the terrible labour of the skiver's job? finishing of ends and edges and preliminary work on the bilge are done with the electric plane.

So two trades have disappeared into oblivion. But a new one has been born: that of the *nuanceur* or blender.

We have already observed that the business of barrel-making is no longer commonplace, but has become a sort of luxury handicraft, strictly the reserve of good wines and quality liqueurs. Visiting wineries is a refinement now open to large numbers of people. It follows that the presentation of a cask or a barrel, formerly confined to ill-lit cellars and firmly closed warehouses, has now taken on its own importance. One more step towards fashion — why, we even use the word robe to speak of a barrel's outer hull.

The master-cooper, then, needs the assistance of the blender, and may even have to rely on a colleague with a better eye than his own. This is no mere luxury. It is plain, pragmatic common sense. Take the perfectly ordinary, everyday example of the customer who wishes to purchase a dozen barrels. Today's highly economic use of raw materials means that one cubic metre of raw oak will do for two vats or barrels. Even the largest billet is seldom more than four cubic metres, and they reckon on an average volume of three. So an order for twelve articles means using wood from at least two trees. Now like all living things, each tree is unique, with its own shading and even texture. So some of the customer's barrels will be light and some darker, and even perhaps light on one side and dark on the other.

What a touch, and what a delight for host and visitor alike!

It is obviously necessary for the staves to be blended harmoniously. This is the new, major development, and no doubt it would have brought a grin to the faces of the rustic coopers of the past.

Blending is done at the same time as the traditional selecting of staves into wide and narrow, spreading the barrel's resistance over the whole surface.

They still use thirty-two staves to assemble a barrel. They are put together in a single packet and sent on to the assembly shop, which is where time seems suddenly to come to a stop. An eighteenth-century barrel-maker would not feel out of place in this vast, airy workshop.

The sequence is over. The tools seem to catch their breath before setting confidently to work once more

*Like careful surgeon-
barbers of days gone by
when there was time to take
the time for such things,
some master-coopers today
specialise in repairing old
barrels, often veritable
masterpieces
(previous pages)*

*Care and strength are
needed to manipulate the
staves on either side of the
damaged one. One of the
world's rare instances
where one can see in action
the tools of a trade three
thousand years old*

The coopers do everything by hand here, and they are not already worn out by the heavy work of the preparatory operations. This means that assembly is now a rapid, almost feather-light business, more like a stupendous piece of juggling than the heavy labour of someone like Zola's heroes.

But let us not forget that if it is indeed juggling, then the jugglers are among the most finely trained athletes anywhere. A simple glance at the muscles of their arms tells the whole story.

The barrels are assembled by the dozen or more, as indeed they need to be to reach the figure of fifty thousand a year. The circular form still opens them up like flowers. They are rolled about and picked up like ballerinas, piled, stacked, to form new walls or even a triumphal staircase in the wings of some magic theatre stolen from the dream of the Great Barrel-Maker.

And then, almost on their own (such is the impression given by this extraordinary ballet), the barrels line up for heating, each squatting over its own brazier, a new figure in the magical dance, now suddenly luminous like so many surreal lanterns. The steam from the swabbing-out process forms a canopy that reflects the flames. The traditional rope cable gave place a century ago to a hand capstan operating a steel cable. The credit for this more practical and more rapid maritime improvement should probably go to the *carpenteys* of Bordeaux, accustomed as they were to working on gabarres out of the barrel-making season.

Suddenly, the wooden flowers have tightened up and become barrels. The second circular form is put on, but still it is not time for the final hooping. Each barrel now goes back onto the oakcutting-burning brazier, and the interior is "cooked" a second time — in a technique that demands some explanation.

How wood is "cooked"

Wood always used to be considered a "neutral" element, one that was perfectly suited to contain, to preserve and to transport wine. There was never any particular problem where good wine was concerned: a three- or four-year-old barrel was held to be no longer usable, good only to be sold off and put to goodness knows what use. They used oak because experience had shown it to be the most dependable of all woods, and that was all there was to it. Cognac producers had rather more detailed ideas, because the oldest *eau-de-vie* would yield aromas of the forest, of flowers, of vanilla, that were subtle and altogether mysterious. And the link was not hard to find.

Towards the end of the 1970s, as barrel-making was coming back and the taste for good wines was becoming more widespread, science once more came to the aid of taste.

The Œnological Institute of the University of Bordeaux II decided to investigate the question of how the flavour of the wood could affect that of the wine. Using the most sophisticated research techniques available, our front-line œnologists arrived (to cut an extremely elaborate story very short indeed) at scientific proof that the oak barrel is not only a suitable container but also a living "skin" able, under certain conditions, to transmit to the wine something of its own secret and invisible substances. This calls to mind the passage in Saint Paul, where he speaks of those things we can see which are made of things that we can't.

Seguin-Moreau put the experiments decided on by the researchers to the practical test, and showed conclusively that a "prepared" cask is both an accelerator and a catalyst. The preparation in question is an additional "cooking" of the interior of the cask, bringing out the wood's intimate savours and

perfumes in accordance with what the customer wants. It is thus possible to "customise" a cask, adjusting the degree of cooking to bring out particular subtleties of flavour — of which there is an infinite variety. The gradual caramelisation produced over the oak-wood fire is light for wines, more intense for cognacs. All of this requires, as one may well imagine, a quite unusual degree of dexterity and intuition. Watching the near-magical care taken by the cooper during this process, one is tempted to wonder if alchemy is quite as dead as people generally think.

The research continues, ever more sophisticated. The Œnological Institute of the University of Bordeaux II and its "secular" branch at Seguin-Moreau promise that the next ten years will produce abundant discoveries and pleasant surprises.

The finished shell, cooked to perfection, ageless; we can still catch one last fleeting glimpse of the mysterious alchemy.

*The fixed compass, tool of
the first builders, and still
used today to decide exactly
where the end bar should go*

100

But our cask is still being made. While the master of the fires continues with his cooking, the ends are assembled — always by hand, the half-staves joined one by one with wooden gudgeon pins and each joint wedged tight with a river reed, just as from time immemorial. Ours is a fabulously inventive age, but no better method has yet been found and that's all there is to it. Our robots can do anything — except make casks, and that is certainly a comfort.

The assembled ends are trimmed and chamfered at the same time by a special machine known by the disarmingly simple name, an end-trimmer.

The chime and the chamfer, that took so much time and trouble in the past, are also done on one very large machine into which the cask actually has to be inserted, known as a *rogneuse-double* or double-trimmer. (It takes a particularly skilled machine-tool operator to maintain the blades.) The cask, now a luxury item as we have seen, is ready for planing and fine sanding. It gets a final ablution before the ends, also sanded, are put on. The first still goes on with the mallet, and the second continues to be inserted at an angle and then hauled into place with the traditional hook-cum-brace: nothing at all new here.

And then it is hooping-time. The age-old operations follow each other in strict order. Hooping is of course still done by hand, for it is common knowledge that if the bilge is the soul of a cask, then the hoops are its life.

And so the master-cooper's dance gets under way again, leaping and prancing, filled with secret balance. It is as if the punches run themselves around the hoops, as they pull the fibres of the staves tighter and ever tighter.

Today, it is no longer a matter of one man or two "sounding" the cask in a gloomy, cluttered lean-to workshop, but rather fifteen or

Apparent confusion, but in fact carefully orchestrated. Each barrel is numbered, stave by stave and hoop by hoop, and then taken apart like some Gothic architectural construction…
(following pages)

101

twenty men wielding muscled arms in the light made dusty by fresh sawdust. It is like the crashing finale to a symphony by Wagner.

As the silence and the sawdust settle together, the end bars are put on, held in place in the time-honoured way with small wedges driven into the chime and fixed with small copper nails. (A luxury item must, after all, be allowed its fripperies.) Last of all, the chestnut hoops go on. They are trimmed and attached with very thin wire before being bound with osier — another time-honoured technique. This last is a particularity of Bordeaux barrels, used therefore for wine, and is immediately followed by the traditional inscription of the manufacturer's signature on the end of the barrel, on a main stave.

It only remains now to drill the bung-hole, which is of course done by hand. And one more barrel joins the line of fifty thousand a year — Seguin-Moreau's figure, and one quarter of all the barrels made in France.

By comparison with the violence and uproar where the casks are made, the two neighbouring workshops appear almost empty, calm, even solemn places, like the bassoon in the cooper's noisy brass band. This is where the tun makers work, turning out the various different models of vats.

The squaring and angling of the vast staves, those ancient and bothersome requirements, are now done on huge planing-machines. Everything else proceeds exactly as it has done for centuries, following a method like that of the cathedral-building roof-carpenters' fraternity. The vat or vats are built in the workshop with one "cooking" and perhaps a second, just like the barrels next door. Each piece is numbered and then dismantled, and the whole thing is taken off to be reassembled on site where the customer wants it. Hooping is a two-man affair, one holding

the long-handled punch, the other wielding the mallet.

On a very large vat, the hoops are so heavy that it takes a winch to lift them above the staves before they are punched into place. Even the heaviest of these monster barrels, which can be of more than 10,000 hectolitres' capacity, can be put together by a specialist team in half a day: and this in spite of the difficulties of the work itself and the often cramped conditions deep inside a wine warehouse. Merpins produces a hundred or so giant vats a year.

OLD TOOLS FOR OLD VATS

It would be wrong to assume that the traditional tools are to be seen only in museum showcases. Seguin-Moreau has a large

...to be reassembled on the other side of the world by a travelling master-cooper

In the wine warehouses, the oaks-turned-barrels have a new static lease of life, carrying a double load: wine, and the ingenuity of man

repair workshop. Hundred-year-old vats and other odd items, very dear to the hearts of their owners, turn up here from everywhere.

Trimmed and assembled sometimes centuries ago, they can only be repaired and given a new lease of useful life by means of the traditional tools. This is why the repair shop has bottom and top planes, jabler saws and Stockholms, adzes and other tools, handled by masters on often amazing pieces. The most remarkable article to be restored in the repair shop in recent years was a sculpted keg from Alsace made in 1680.

In view of all the foregoing, one might well expect to be moved by the sight of a new cask — the exact replica of the barrels of Silenus or Diogenes, the sum of several thousand years of acquired skills.

The new barrel is indeed basically identical. It may be rather less rough, somewhat "better-bred" than its ancient fellows. But the primary use to which it is put has not altered. Our highly scientific age can improve, but not innovate. It is like having the latest Ferrari side-by-side with the Model T Ford at a motor show, the only difference being that the cars have less than a century between them.

However traditional it may be, the modern cask is also the fruit of a different, very arduous, train of thought: how to reduce the difficulty of the work involved. Construction details are thus better understood. The raw materials are used more economically. The shape is more effortlessly perfect, the finished object has more regularity.

It is this new uniformity which has enabled the Œnological Institute of the University of Bordeaux II to complete its first research phase, making possible whole series of experiments (the only means to a scientific conclusion).

A "family" photograph at Seguin-Moreau. (following pages)

It is no mere happy chance that Seguin-Moreau barrels are exported all over the world. It is the result of a remarkable capacity for adaptation, rather like that of leading fashion designers. It is obvious to the naked eye that, for them, no two customers are the same.

For the barrel-makers of Merpins, no two wines are the same, even if they are the produce of the same family of vinestocks. The great wines of France, for example, the clarets, the Burgundies, the Cognacs, are made from different vinestock planted together, the mixture giving results that are well known. In the U.S.A., on the other hand, or in Australia and New Zealand, the wines are usually made from a single vinestock, planted somewhat crudely.

It is on the basis of these other flavours that local consumer tastes and behaviour develop, and casks are needed that are suited to these variations. One is easily led to suspect that perfect casks, perfectly "prepared" to magnify the virtues of a particular harvest, even from the Antipodes, are of special appeal to *grand cru* producers.

It is true that such producers are understandably proud to display to visitors series of barrels stamped with the Seguin-Moreau seal. Merpins barrels and casks are to be found in the USA and in Chile, in Germany and in New Zealand, in Australia, in Italy — and even in Japan: but this is just in order to refine imported products to the Japanese taste. It certainly seems that, thanks to the modern barrel, the entire world is acquiring a taste for wine.

Even with all the developments, though, if the dugout canoe paddler of the beginning of our story were to reappear in our midst today, born as he was at a time of unsophisticated, little-changing customs and tools, he would certainly not be terribly surprised at the universal application to which his invention has been put.

Printed in Spain.
March 1995
© Seguin Moreau, 1991
ISBN: 2-87938-000-6

Design and layout: Thomas Gravemaker
Coordination and production: Isabelle Gruffaz
Photo-engraving: Prodima S.A., Spain
Printing: Castuera, S.A., Spain

Editions de la Presqu'île, 15, rue de la Cité, 33310 Lormont